**INTRO TO PHYSICS** Need to Know

SilverTip

# Electricity

by Jane Parks Gardner

Consultant: Kathy Renfrew
Science Educator and Science Learner

Minneapolis, Minnesota

## Credits

Cover and title page, © Muhammah Haseeb/Shutterstock; 5T, © CentralITAlliance/iStock; 5C, © blackred/iStock; 5B, © Semmick Photo/Shutterstock; 7, © Filip Miletic/Shutterstock; 9, © Filip Miletic/Shutterstock; 11, © Roman Samborskyi/Shutterstock; 13T, © aquaArts studio/iStock; 13B, © Gwoeii/Shutterstock; 14–15, © Pau Buera/Shutterstock; 17, © Soonthorn Wongsaita/Shutterstock; 18, © Andrey_Popov/Shutterstock; 19, © ESB Basic/Shutterstock; 21, © Sergey Ryzhov/Shutterstock; 23, © Jenari/Shutterstock; 25, © fen deneyim/Shutterstock; 26–27, © Herr Loeffler/Shutterstock; 28T, © Vector FX/Shutterstock; and 28B, © gritsalak karalak/Shutterstock.

## Bearport Publishing Company Product Development Team

President: Jen Jenson; Director of Product Development: Spencer Brinker; Senior Editor: Allison Juda; Editor: Charly Haley; Associate Editor: Naomi Reich; Senior Designer: Colin O'Dea; Associate Designer: Elena Klinkner; Product Development Assistant: Anita Stasson

Library of Congress Cataloging-in-Publication Data is available at www.loc.gov or upon request from the publisher.

ISBN: 979-8-88509-220-3 (hardcover)
ISBN: 979-8-88509-227-2 (paperback)
ISBN: 979-8-88509-234-0 (ebook)

Copyright © 2023 Bearport Publishing Company. All rights reserved. No part of this publication may be reproduced in whole or in part, stored in any retrieval system, or transmitted in any form or by any means, electronic, mechanical, photocopying, recording, or otherwise, without written permission from the publisher.

For more information, write to Bearport Publishing, 5357 Penn Avenue South, Minneapolis, MN 55419. Printed in the United States of America.

# Contents

A World of Electricity . . . . . . . . . . 4

All about Atoms . . . . . . . . . . . . . . 6

Making Movement . . . . . . . . . 10

A Big Shock . . . . . . . . . . . . . . 14

Electricity We Use . . . . . . . . . . . 16

Keeping It Current . . . . . . . . . . . 18

Flip That Switch . . . . . . . . . . . . 22

Battery Powered . . . . . . . . . . . . 24

Energy Everywhere . . . . . . . . . . . 26

Static Electricity . . . . . . . . . . . . . . . 28

SilverTips for Success . . . . . . . . . . . . 29

Glossary . . . . . . . . . . . . . . . . . . 30

Read More . . . . . . . . . . . . . . . . 31

Learn More Online . . . . . . . . . . . . . 31

Index . . . . . . . . . . . . . . . . . . . 32

About the Author . . . . . . . . . . . . . . 32

# A World of Electricity

Electricity sends your fan spinning. It can make sound come out of your speakers. And sometimes electricity heats or lights up a whole room. A lightning bolt streaking across the sky is electricity, too.

But just what is electricity? It's **energy**.

There are many kinds of energy. In addition to electrical energy, these include chemical, heat, and mechanical energy. Energy can't be created or destroyed. But it can be changed from one form to another.

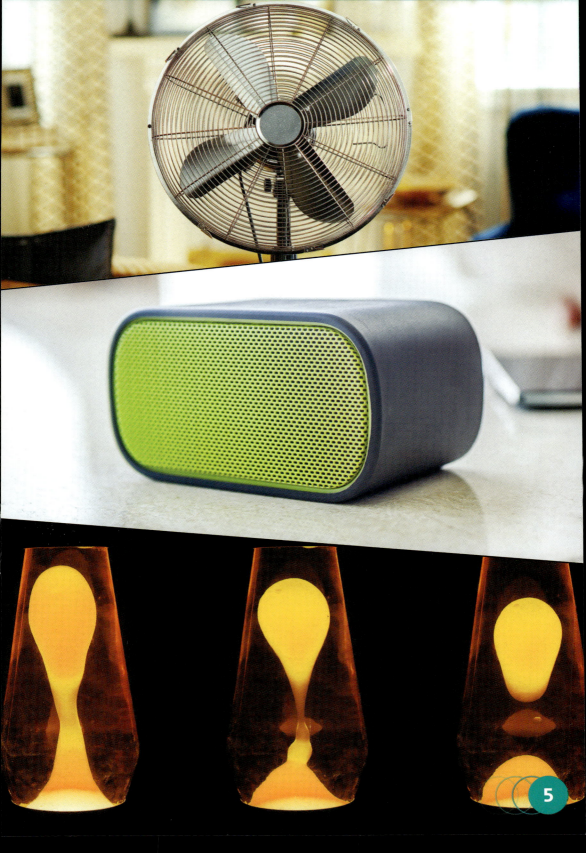

# All about Atoms

All that electrical energy starts with something very, very small.

Everything is made of tiny **atoms**. And atoms are made of even smaller parts. A nucleus at the center of the atom has **protons** and neutrons. **Electrons** move around the nucleus.

Electrons spin around the nucleus extremely fast. Because of this, scientists can only guess where they are at any given time.

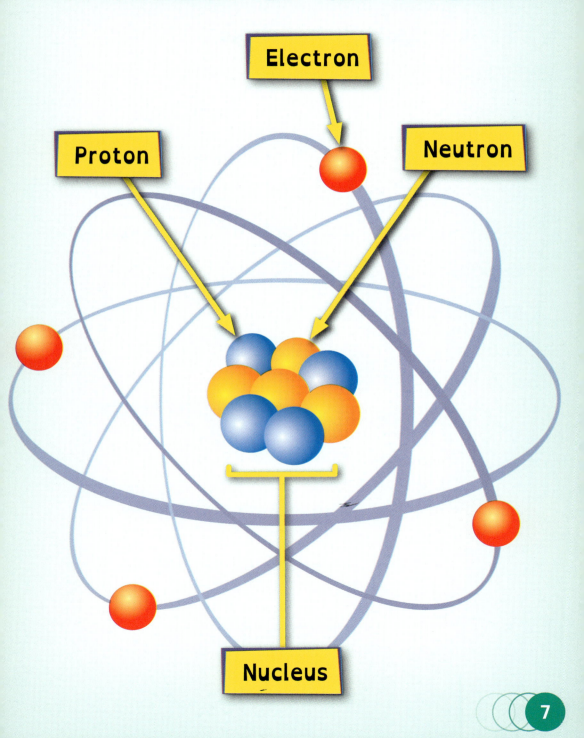

Some of these parts have a charge. Protons have a positive charge, and electrons have a negative charge. Usually, atoms have the same number of protons as electrons. This makes them neutral. But sometimes atoms lose an electron or two. These electrons on the move make electricity.

Neutrons in the nucleus don't have a charge. They are neutral. Like all parts of an atom, we can't see them. But scientists know they must be neutral because of the way atoms behave.

# Charges in an Atom

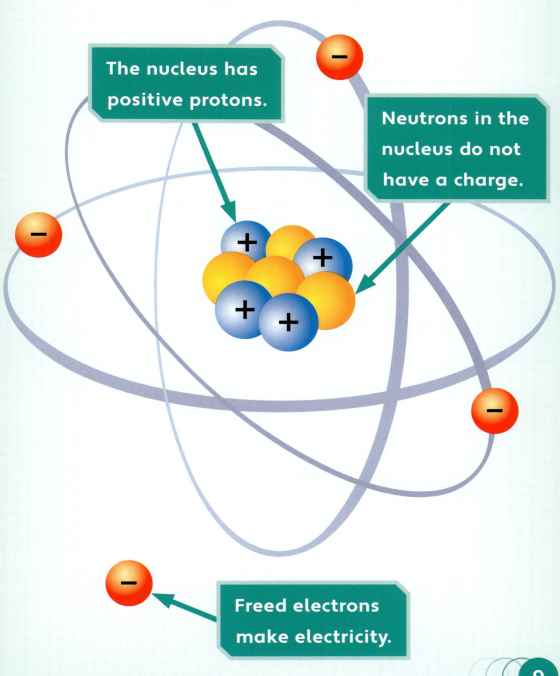

# Making Movement

Adding energy to an object can make electrons move. If you rub a balloon against your shirt, you add energy. Electrons move from the shirt to the balloon. Then, the balloon will have a negative charge with more electrons than protons. Your shirt will have a few more protons, so it will be positive.

Opposite charges attract. Negative electrons are attracted to, or drawn toward, positive protons. And protons are attracted to electrons.

Be careful about what happens next. You might get zapped, thanks to electricity. **Static electricity** is the buildup of a charge in one place. When this happens, atoms work to become neutral again. Negatively charged electrons flow toward a positively charged object. This causes the shock you get.

You can feel, see, and hear static electricity. It may zap you. It is also the crackling you hear when you pull apart laundry fresh from the dryer. You may see it as a spark, too.

# A Big Shock

Lightning makes a much larger zap. But it, too, is the release of static electricity. Water drops in a cloud rub together. This makes electrons build up on the bottom of the cloud. Once enough of them are there, they head toward protons on the ground. *Crack!*

Lightning is electrical energy with light. But its energy makes a lot of heat, too. In fact, a lightning bolt can be five times hotter than the surface of the sun!

# Electricity We Use

Lightning bolts are full of electricity. But we can't use them to power our homes. We get that electricity from other forms of energy. Sometimes, we burn fossil fuels to create energy that makes electricity. We can also use energy from the wind or sun to make electricity.

When fossil fuels are gone, that's it. But wind and sunshine will always be around. So, many people are trying to use more of these kinds of energy for electricity.

# Keeping It Current

How do we get electricity to go where we want it? With **current electricity**, we make electrons flow in one direction from one place to another. Just as water flows through a hose, we direct electrons along a current.

Electrons flow through wires in your walls to your plugged-in TV. This flowing electrical energy becomes power so you can watch a show.

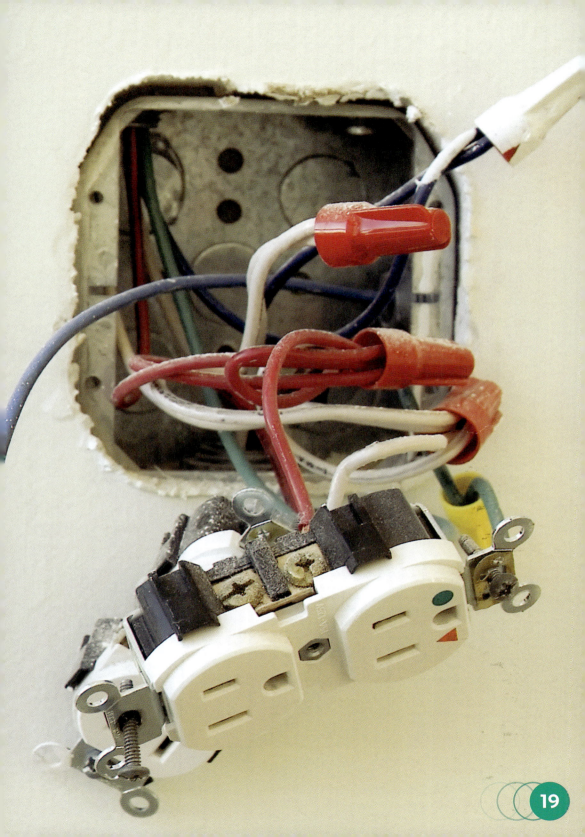

Electrons in a current flow along a **circuit**. This path for moving electricity is usually made of metal wires. Why metal? Metals are good **conductors**. They allow electrons to easily pass through them.

How do we stop an electric current in wires from going where we don't want it to? The wires are coated in plastics or other **insulators**. These keep electrons from flowing where they shouldn't.

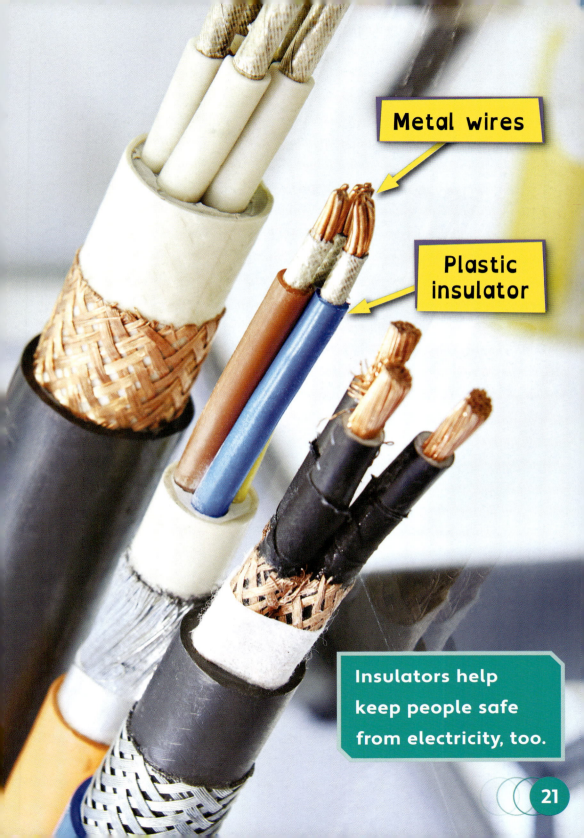

# Flip That Switch

We make circuits to create a flow of electricity. But we can just as easily stop it. Turning off a light switch breaks the circuit. Then, electrons cannot run through the wire in a current. Flip that switch again and the current flows. You can see light!

Why bother breaking a circuit? If we do, we aren't wasting electricity we do not need. This saves energy.

# Battery Powered

Electricity can be stored, too. It can be changed into chemical energy and kept in a battery. This energy is slowly released when it is connected to a circuit. Push the button on a flashlight to turn on its circuit. Then, you can see thanks to the flow of electricity.

Batteries have a positive end and a negative end. Electrons build up on the negative end. When you turn the device on, electrons begin to flow through the circuit to get back to the positive end.

# Energy Everywhere

Electricity powers a dryer and makes clothes stick together when they are freshly dried. The movement of electrons lights up our lives, brings us heat, and keeps us moving. Energy is everywhere. You just have to know how to use it!

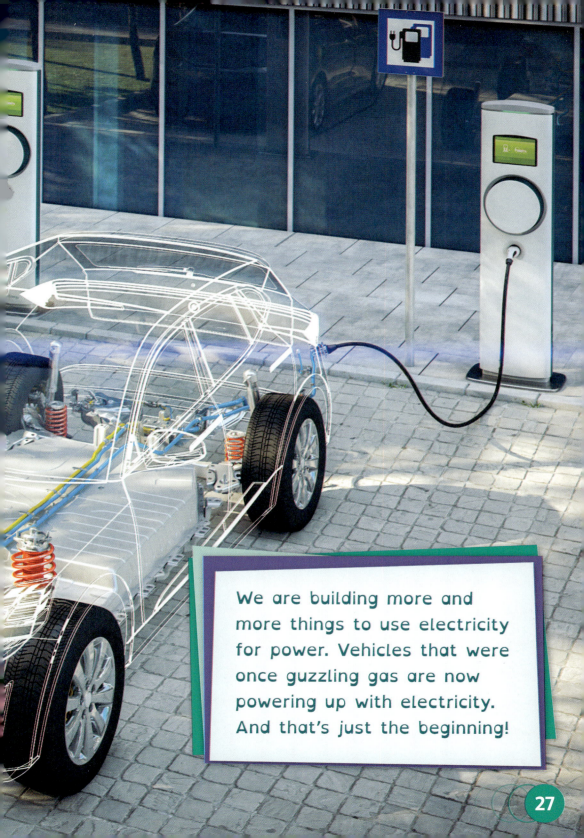

We are building more and more things to use electricity for power. Vehicles that were once guzzling gas are now powering up with electricity. And that's just the beginning!

# Static Electricity

Most of the time, atoms have a neutral charge. They have the same number of electrons and protons.

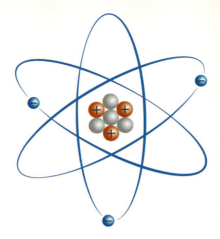

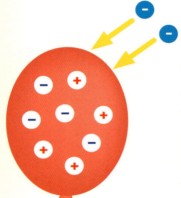

When energy is transferred to an object, electrons may begin to move.

Rubbing a balloon on your head causes electrical energy to build up.

Your hair has a positive charge and the balloon has a negative charge. They are attracted to each other.

28

# SilverTips for SUCCESS

## ★ SilverTips for REVIEW

Review what you've learned. Use the text to help you.

### Define key terms

atom
charge
circuit
current electricity
static electricity

### Check for understanding

What are the three parts of an atom and what charges do they hold?

Where does static electricity get its energy from?

Describe how a circuit works.

### Think deeper

Explain the similarities and differences between static electricity and current electricity.

---

## ★ SilverTips on TEST-TAKING

- **Make a study plan.** Ask your teacher what the test is going to cover. Then, set aside time to study a little bit every day.

- **Read all the questions carefully.** Be sure you know what is being asked.

- **Skip any questions** you don't know how to answer right away. Mark them and come back later if you have time.

# Glossary

**atoms** the tiny building blocks that make up every substance in the universe

**circuit** the path that electricity flows along

**conductors** materials that electricity can flow through

**current electricity** electricity that moves through a circuit

**electrons** tiny parts of atoms that carry negative electrical charges

**energy** the ability to do work, or cause changes

**insulators** materials that electricity cannot flow through

**protons** tiny parts of an atom that carry positive electric charges

**static electricity** an imbalance of electric charges

# Read More

**Crane, Cody.** *Electricity and Magnetism (A True Book: Physical Science).* New York: Children's Press, 2019.

**Linde, Barbara Martina.** *Electric Currents: It's Energetic (Spotlight on Physical Science).* New York: PowerKids Press, 2020.

**Swanson, Jennifer.** *How Does Electricity Work? (Explaining How Things Work).* Mankato, MN: The Child's World, 2022.

# Learn More Online

1. Go to **www.factsurfer.com** or scan the QR code below.
2. Enter **"Physics Electricity"** into the search box.
3. Click on the cover of this book to see a list of websites.

# Index

**atoms** 6–9, 12, 28

**battery** 24

**circuit** 20, 22, 24

**conductor** 20

**current** 18, 20, 22

**energy** 4, 6, 10, 14, 16, 18, 22, 24, 26, 28

**fossil fuels** 16

**insulator** 20–21

**lightning** 4, 14, 16

**neutrons** 6–9

**protons** 6–10, 14, 28

**static electricity** 12, 14, 28

# About the Author

Jane Parks Gardner has written more than 50 nonfiction books. Jane spends a lot of her time thinking about, reading about, writing about, and talking about science to anyone who'll listen.